Simple Amharic For Adoptive Families

By Amy Kendall

Copyright © 2008
Amy Kendall

"God sets the lonely
in families."

Psalm 68:6

Contents

Acknowledgements

I am grateful to Mengist Teshale for his attentive work on the written translation of the words and phrases in this book. I am certain that his time and effort will be a great blessing to adoptive families who use this resource to help welcome their child home. He also deserves recognition for his great voice work on the recording. It was truly a joy to work with him on this project.

I also want to express my gratitude to Duni Zenaye for taking the time to proof read the manuscript and to offer her thoughts and suggestions. I warmly thank her for her invaluable input.

Introduction

Congratulations as you walk on the beautiful road towards adoption! As a fellow adoptive mom I understand the reality of falling head over heels for a little person that you hardly even know. I know about long waits and set backs. I know about living in anticipation for the moment when your family will all be in one place!

I can understand how it feels to prepare for the transition that will take place in my life, but I can't even begin to try to put myself in the shoes of a child who enters a new family in a distant land. There are different foods, different caretakers, different sleeping arrangements, different clothes, and on top of that the unfamiliar sounds of a foreign language. Most confident adults would crumble under these conditions! For a child who is too little to be in control of his or her surroundings it must be a very uncomfortable experience to say the least.

This book was written with the great hope of making that transition a bit easier for the new child in your family. Hopefully these words and phrases in your child's native language will give you a way to explain things to help ease their fears, keep them safe, and most importantly, to let them know how very much you love them.

Amy Kendall

How to Use This Book

Baby steps, baby steps:

As they say, "Rome wasn't built in a day." In the same way, learning your Amharic words may take some patience. Take it a little at a time, section by section, and pretty soon you'll notice that some of it is starting to stick.

Read and listen:

At first you may want to sit down and listen to the CD and read along in your book (it helps if you can sit on a comfy couch and sip a latté). This book was created with the great hope of making Amharic very easy for you and your family. Begin by following along with the phonetic pronunciations and familiarizing yourself with the material.

Don't be shy:

After you have a feel for what you will be learning, pop the CD in at home or in your car and try to mimic each word or phrase in the spaces that have been provided. When what you say holds no resemblance to the Amharic on the CD, throw your head back and have a good laugh. Encourage those around you to do the same. Everyone has to start somewhere and we should never take ourselves too seriously.

Use it:

Start incorporating the words and phrases into your daily life. When you sit down at a meal and take your first bite, announce that the food is *Yee-TAHF-tahl!*. Shower family members with words of love and affection in Amharic (don't forget your spouse)! Everyone likes hearing how special they are…any language will do. Send your children to find their *CHAH-mah* and see what they bring back. If you don't have children in your home yet, throw in a little challenge to spice things up. The person who can incorporate the most Amharic words and phrases into their day gets treated to a meal at their favorite restaurant (loser pays)! Since waiting each month for your child can feel like 1,000 years, your family may just be a few stops short of crazy anyway. Some activities like these might be a welcome diversion!

Flip it:

Quiz yourself (this is for you type "A's"). The book is wire bound so that you can fold the pages back on one another to create flash cards ("How *convenient!*" you exclaim). Look at the English words and phrases and see if you can remember their Amharic equivalents without looking.

Finally, give yourself a break:

If you have ever been in a situation where you are the only English speaker and everyone around you is chatting away in another language, you know how lonely it can be. When someone makes an attempt to communicate with you (be

4

it ever so feebly!) you feel nothing but appreciation. Likewise, your child will surely see through all of your mistakes and blunders, straight into a heart that cares and is overflowing with love for them. So, give it a try and don't worry about perfection.

Amharic Notes

* English speakers are accustomed to addressing everyone with the same words whether we are speaking to our pet hamster, or to a person of great honor. However, it should be noted that Amharic makes a distinction between a formal and informal address. Since this book is written to help you communicate with children, we have used the informal form in all of the phrases. Do not use this form when you communicate with an adult, especially an adult who is older than you and should be treated with respect.

* As you begin to learn your Amharic words and phrases, you will inevitably encounter some sounds that you have never tried to make with your mouth before. For instance, Amharic has a "K" sound that sounds a bit like you are clearing your throat (we have written it as "KH"). Please don't be thrown by these new sounds! We have tried to come as close as we can in our written pronunciations. However, your CD will be your best friend in this area.

* Most of your phrases will change depending on whether you are speaking *to a boy* (B) or *to a girl* (G). We have repeated the phrase two times in the phrases where gender does not matter simply to give you some extra practice.

1. Coming Home

1. I am your Mommy.

2. I am your Daddy.

3. This is your sister.

4. This is your brother.

1. (B) Eh-NAY eh-NAH-tekh negn.
   (G) Eh-NAY eh-NAH-tish negn.

2. (B) Eh-NAY ah-BAH-tekh negn.
   (G) Eh-NAY ah-BAH-tish negn.

3. (B) Ee-CHEE eh-HEH-tekh naht.
   (G) Ee-CHEE eh-HEH-tish naht.

4. (B) Yih-HEH won-dih-MIKH nohw.
   (G) Yih-HEH won-dih-MISH nohw.

5. You are my daughter.

6. You are my son.

7. You are going to live with us.

8. You are going to live with me.

5. Ahn-CHEE lee-JAY nesh.

6. Ahn-TEH lee-JAY nekh.

7. (B) Ahn-TEH keh-GNAH gahr nohw
      yeh-mih-TNOH-row.
   (G) Ahn-CHEE keh-GNAH gahr nohw
      yeh-mih-TNOHR-rew.

8. (B) Ahn-TEH keh-NAY gahr nohw
      yeh-mih-TNOH-row.
   (G) Ahn-CHEE keh-NAY gahr nohw
      yeh-mih-TNOHR-rew.

9. We will take good care of you.

10. I will take good care of you.

11. We are so happy to be your family.

9. (B) Beh-DENB ten-keh-bahk-BEN
        eh-nah-SAH-dig-ih-HAH-lehn.
   (G) Beh-DENB ten-keh-bahk-BEN
        eh-nah-SAH-dig-ih-SHAH-lehn.

10. (B) Beh-DENB ten-keh-bah-keh-BAY
        eh-yih-zih-HAH-loh.
    (G) Beh-DENB ten-keh-bah-keh-BAY
        eh-yih-zih-SHAH-loh.

11. (B) Yeh-GNAH beh-teh-SEHB
        ah-BAHL beh-meh-HOH-neh
        des bloh-gnal.
    (G) Yeh-GNAH beh-teh-SEHB
        ah-BAHL beh-meh-HOH-nesh
        des bloh-gnal.

11

12. I am so happy to be your family.

13. We love you so much!

14. I love you so much!

15. You are so precious.

16. Don't be afraid.

12. (B) Yeh-beh-teh-SEHB ah-BAHL
       seh-leh-HONK des bloh-GNAL.
    (G) Yeh-beh-teh-SEHB ah-BAHL
       seh-leh-HONSH des bloh-GNAL.

13. (B) Beht-AHM ehn-wuh-dih-HAH-lehn!
    (G) Beht-AHM ehn-wuh-dih-SHAH-lehn!

14. (B) Beht-AHM ehn-wuh-dih-HAH-loh!
    (G) Beht-AHM ehn-wuh-dih-SHAH-loh!

15. (B) Ahn-TEH WUH-deh nekh.
    (G) Ahn-CHEE WUH-deh nesh.

16. (B) AH-teh-frah.
    (G) AH-teh-free.

17. Don't worry.

18. It's OK.

19. I am with you.

20. Can I hold you?

21. We are going to ride on an airplane!

22. We're going to ride in a car.

17. (B) Ah-TAH-sehb.
    (G) Ah-TAH-seh-bee.

18. MIH-nim EYE-dehl.

19. (B) Eh-NAY ah-beh-RAYKH negn.
    (G) Eh-NAY ah-beh-RESH negn.

20. (B) Lay-ah-ZEKH?
    (G) Lay-ah-ZESH?

21. Beh-ah-roh-PLAHN nohw
    yeh-min-HEH-doh!

22. Beh-meh-kee-NAH nohw
    yeh-min-HEH-doh.

23. This is your car seat.

24. We'll be there soon.

23. (B) Yikh yahn-TEH
       meh-keh-meh-CHAH nohw.
    (G) Yikh yahn-CHEE
       meh-keh-meh-CHAH nohw.

24. Ah-HOON ehn-dehr-SAH-lehn.

2. At the Table

1. Are you hungry?

2. Do you want to eat?

3. Do you want a drink?

4. Let's eat!

5. Do you like it?

1. (B) Rah-BEKH?
   (G) Rah-BESH?

2. (B) Meh-blaht tih-fuh-lih-GAHL-ekh?
   (G) Meh-blaht tih-fuh-lih-GAL-esh?

3. (B) Mee-teh-TAH tih-fuh-lih-GAHL-ekh?
   (G) Mee-teh-TAH tih-fuh-lih-GAL-esh?

4. Eh-NEH-blah!

5. (B) Wuh-DEHD-kow?
   (G) Wuh-DEHD-shew?

19

6. Delicious!

7. Do you want more?

8. Are you finished?

9. We'll have more later.

10. Do you want...?

11. Juice

6. Yee-TAHF-tahl!

7. (B) Yee-cheh-meh-RAH-lekh?
   (G) Yee-cheh-meh-RAH-lesh?

8. (B) Chah-RESK?
   (G) Chah-RESH?

9. Beh-huh-AH-lah ehn-cheh-meh-RAH-lehn.

10. (B) ...tih-fuh-lih-GAHL-ekh?
    (G) ...tih-fuh-lih-GAL-esh?
(Insert the direct object at the beginning of the sentence.)

11. Chee-MAH-kee

12. Water

13. Milk

14. Snack

15. Bottle

12. WUH-hah

13. WUH-teht

14. MEHK-sehs

15. TOO-toh

3. Bathroom

1. Do you need to go potty?

2. Do you need me to change your diaper?

3. Poo poo

4. Pee pee

24

1. (B) Meh-tah-tih-bee-yah BAYT
   meh-HEHD tih-fuh-lih-GAHL-ekh?
   (G) Meh-tah-tih-bee-yah-BAYT
   meh-HEHD tih-fuh-lih-GAL-esh?

2. (B) Shint chehr-keh-HEN
   leh-keh-YIR-lekh?
   (G) Shint chehr-keh-SHEN
   leh-keh-YIR-lesh?

3. KAH-kah

4. Shint

5. Please don't go potty in your pants.

6. I will find a bathroom.

7. Do you need help?

8. Can you do it by yourself?

9. I will help you.

5. (B) LIB-seh lie ah-tish-NAH.
   (G) LIB-sesh lie ah-tish-GNEE.

6. Shint bayt ih-fuh-lih-GAH-loh.

7. (B) Ehr-DAH-tah tih-fuh-lih-GAHL-ekh?
   (G) Ehr-DAH-tah tih-fuh-lih-GAL-esh?

8. (B) Rah-sih-HIN cheh-LEKH
      tah-dir-geh-WAH-lekh?
   (G) Rah-sih-SHIN cheh-LESH
      tah-dir-geh-WAH-lesh?

9. (B) Eh-reh-dah-HAH-loh.
   (G) Eh-reh-dah-SHAH-loh.

10. Let's wash your hands.

10. (B) Eh-jeh-HIHN ih-NIT-ah-bow.
    (G) Eh-jeh-SHIN ih-NIT-ah-bow.

4. Personal Care

1. Are you hot?

2. Are you cold?

3. It's time to take a bath.

4. Let's brush your teeth.

1. (B) Moh-KEKH?
   (G) Moh-KESH?

2. (B) Beh-REH-dekh?
   (G) Beh-REH-desh?

3. Soh-NEHT meh-TAH-teh-beh-AH
   seh-AHT nohw.

4. (B) Tir-sih-HIN eh-nih-FAK.
   (G) Tir-sih-SHIN eh-nih-FAK.

5. Let's comb your hair.

6. Let's trim your nails.

7. Let's get dressed.

8. Let's go!

5. (B) Tsah-GUHR-hin eh-NAH-bet-row.
   (G) Tsah-GUHR-ih-shin eh-NAH-bet-row.

6. (B) TUH-frih-hin eh-noo-GRAHT.
   (G) TUH-frih-shin eh-noo-GRAHT.

7. Eh-NIL-behs.

8. Eh-NIH-hid!

5. Playtime

1. Let's play!

2. Would you like to go and play?

3. Would you like to go outside and play?

1. Eh-NICH-ah-wuht!

2. (B) Hee-DEH meh-CHAH-wuht
      tih-fuh-lih-GAHL-ekh?
   (G) Hee-DESH meh-CHAH-wuht
      tih-fuh-lih-GAL-esh?

3. (B) Witch woh-TEKH meh-CHAH-wuht
      tih-fuh-lih-GAHL-ekh?
   (G) Witch woh-TESH meh-CHAH-wuht
      tih-fuh-lih-GAL-esh?

4. Please share.

5. Please give it back.

6. Good job!

7. Please clean up.

8. You are a good helper!

9. Toys

4. (B) Eh-bah-KIKH tuh-KAH-fehl.
   (G) Eh-bah-KISH tuh-KAH-feh-ee.

5. (B) Eh-bah-KIKH MEH-lis.
   (G) Eh-bah-KISH MEH-lih-shee.

6. Tih-ROO sih-RAH!

7. (B) Eh-bah-KIKH AH-seh-dah.
   (G) Eh-bah-KISH AH-seh-jee.

8. (B) Tih-ROO rah-DAH-hegn!
   (G) Tih-ROO rah-DAH-sheen!

9. Ah-SHAHN-goo-leet

10. Ball

11. Car

10. Kwahs

11. My-KEE-nah

6. Bedtime

1. Are you tired?

2. It's naptime.

3. Time for bed.

4. Let's pray.

5. Sweet dreams.

1. (B) Deh-keh-MEKH?
   (G) Deh-keh-MESH?

2. Yeh-ihn-KILF seh-AHT nohw.

3. Yeh-MIH-gneh-tah seh-AHT nohw.

4. Ihn-TSAH-lay.

5. Mehl-KAHM ehn-KULF.

6. I'll sing you a song.

7. Night, night.

8. See you in the morning!

9. Please lay quietly in your bed.

10. Did you have a bad dream?

6. (B) Mehz-MOHR eh-zah-MEHR-leh-hah-loh.
   (G) Mehz-MOHR eh-zah-MEHR-lish-ah-loh.

7. Mah-TAH, mah-TAH.

8. (B) Twaht ah-yih-HAH-loh!
   (G) Twaht ah-yih-SHAH-loh!.

9. (B) Eh-bah-KIKH tsaht bih-LEH
      GAH-dehm behl.
   (G) Eh-bah-KISH tsaht bih-LESH
      GAH-dehm bay.

10. (B) Meht-FOH hilm ah-YEKH?
    (G) Meht-FOH hilm ah-YESH?

11. Do you want me to stay with you a little bit?

12. Is it too dark?

13. Do you want me to leave the light on?

14. Blanket

15. Book

16. Pillow

11. (B) Tih-NISH AH-breh lih-KOY?
    (G) Tih-NISH AH-bresh lih-KOY?

12. Beht-AHM cheh-leh-MAH nohw?

13. Meh-BRAH-too ehn-deh-beh-RAH
    yih-KOY?

14. BIRD-libs

15. Meh-sih-HAF

16. Tih-RAHS

7. Health

1. Are you sick?

2. Where does it hurt?

3. Point to where it hurts.

4. I'm sorry you don't feel well.

1. (B) Ah-MEH-mekh?
   (G) Ah-MEH-mesh?

2. (B) Yeht lie nohw yah-mih-MEKH?
   (G) Yeht lie nohw yah-mih-MESH?

3. (B) Yah-meh-mih-HIN boh-TAH
      ah-sah-YEGN?
   (G) Yah-meh-mih-SHIN boh-TAH
      ah-sah-YEGN?

4. (B) Seh-lah-meh-MEKH ahz-NAH-loh.
   (G) Seh-lah-meh-MESH ahz-NAH-loh.

47

5. Are you OK?

6. Owie or wound

7. May I kiss it?

8. I'll get a bandaid.

9. This is the doctor.

10. This will make you feel better.

5. (B) Teh-SHAH-lekh?
   (G) Teh-SHAH-lesh?

6. KOO-sil

7. Lih-SAHM-ow?

8. (B) PLAH-stehr ah-meht-ah-leh-HAH-loh.
   (G) PLAH-stehr ah-meht-ah-leh-SHAH-loh.

9. Yikh hah-KIM nohw.

10. (B) Yikh yah-SHIH-leh-hahl.
    (G) Yikh yah-SHIH-leh-shahl.

11. This is a shot.

12. This might hurt a little, but I will be here with you.

13. This won't hurt.

11. (B) Yikh yeh-mih-teh-wuh-GAOW
mehr-FAY nohw.
(G) Yikh yeh-mih-teh-wuh-GAOW
mehr-FAY nohw.

12. (B) Tih-NISH yah-meh-HAHL gihn
eh-NAY ah-bih-RAY AH-loh.
(G) Tih-NISH yah-meh-SHAHL gihn
eh-NAY ah-bih-RAY AH-loh.

13. Yikh ah-yah-MIM.

8. Words of Affection and Assurance

1. I love you.

2. I will always love you.

3. You are so special!

4. You are so smart!

1. (B) Eh-wuh-dih-HAH-loh.
   (G) Eh-wuh-dih-SHAH-loh.

2. (B) Hoo-LEHM eh-wuh-dih-HAH-loh.
   (G) Hoo-LEHM eh-wuh-dih-SHAH-loh.

3. (B) Ahn-TEH beht-AHM lee-YOO nekh!
   (G) Ahn-CHEE beht-AHM lee-YOO nesh!

4. (B) Ahn-TEH GOH-behz nekh!
   (G) Ahn-CHEE GOH-behz nesh!

5. You are so handsome!

6. You are so beautiful!

7. I am so proud of you!

8. Can I have a hug?

9. Can I give you a hug?

10. Can I have a kiss?

5. Ahn-TEH beht-AHM kohn-JOH nekh!

6. Ahn-CHEE beht-AHM kohn-JOH nesh!

7. (B) Beht-AHM kohr-OW-bekh!
   (G) Beht-AHM kohr-OW-hoo-bish!

8. (B) Eh-KUH-fegn?
   (G) Eh-KUH-feegn?

9. (B) Lih-KUH-fikh?
   (G) Lih-KUH-fish?

10. (B) Sah-MEGN?
    (G) Sah-MEEGN?

11. Can I give you a kiss?

12. You are wonderful!

13. Rose (loving term for girl)

14. Brave (loving term for boy)

15. My beautiful or my handsome
    (for girl or boy)

16. Dear

11. (B) Lih-SAH-mikh?
    (G) Lih-SAH-mish?

12. (B) Ahs-deh-nah-KEE nekh!
    (G) Ahs-deh-nah-KEE nesh!

13. Tsee-YEH-rih-dah

14. JEH-gih-nohw

15. YEH-nay KOHN-joh

16. (B) Wuhd
    (G) Wuh-DAY

17. Sweetie

18. Sunshine

19. My baby

20. I'll be right back.

21. I'll be back in a little while.

22. I missed you!

17. YEH-nay mahr

18. Tsuh-HYE

19. Yeh-NAY lij

20. Ah-HOON eh-meh-LEH-sah-loh.

21. Kuh-tih-NISH gee-ZAY boh-HAH-lah
    eh-meh-LEH-sah-loh.

22. (B) Nah-fih-keh-HAH-loh!
    (G) Nah-fih-keh-SHAH-loh!

23. I won't leave you.

*Another way to show affection to your child is to add the syllable –yay to the end of their name.

23. (B) Tih-YEKH ahl-HEH-dehm.
    (G) Tih-YESH ahl-HEH-dehm.

9. Boundaries and Directions

1. Please don't do that.

2. Not now, we'll do it later.

3. Wait!

4. Stop!

1. (B) Eh-bah-KIKH ehn-deh-SOO ah-TAHRG.
   (G) Eh-bah-KISH ehn-deh-SOO
       ah-TAHR-gee.

2. Beh-huh-AH-lah ehn-seh-rah-WAH-lehn.

3. (B) Koy!
   (G) KOY-ee!

4. (B) Koom!
   (G) KOOM-ee!

5. Look!

6. Please don't touch.

7. Please don't hit.

8. Please don't bite.

9. Please don't put that in your mouth.

5. (B) Ay!
   (G) AY-ee!

6. (B) Eh-bah-KIKH ah-TEEN-kah.
   (G) Eh-bah-KISH ah-TEEN-kee.

7. (B) Eh-bah-KIKH ah-TIM-tah.
   (G) Eh-bah-KISH ah-TIM-chee.

8. (B) Eh-bah-KIKH ah-TEHN-kehs.
   (G) Eh-bah-KISH ah-TEHN-kesh.

9. (B) Eh-bah-KIKH AH-fih wuhst
       ah-TAHS-geh-bah.
   (G) Eh-bah-KISH AH-fish wuhst
       ah-TAHS-geh-bee.

10. Please don't run.

11. Please don't shout.

12. Please don't push.

13. Sit down.

14. Stand up.

10. (B) Eh-bah-KIKH ah-tih-ROOT.
    (G) Eh-bah-KISH ah-tih-ROOCH.

11. (B) Eh-bah-KIKH ah-tich-OO.
    (G) Eh-bah-KISH ah-tih-choo-HEE.

12. (B) Eh-bah-KIKH ah-TIG-fah.
    (G) Eh-bah-KISH ah-TIG-fee.

13. (B) Tuh-keh-MEHT.
    (G) Tuh-keh-MECH.

14. (B) Tuh-NEH-sah.
    (G) Tuh-NEH-shee.

15. Be careful.

16. Let's hold hands.

17. Stay together.

18. Come here.

19. Go there.

20. Stay close to me.

15. (B) Tuh-TEHN-kekh.
    (G) Tuh-TEHN-keh-KEE.

16. Eh-JAH-chin eh-nay-YAH-yaz.

17. Ah-BREHN eh-nih-KOY.

18. (B) Eh-ZEE nah.
    (G) Eh-ZEE nay.

19. (B) Eh-ZAH heed.
    (G) Eh-ZAH heedj.

20. (B) Eh-NAYN ah-TIL-kuhkh.
    (G) Eh-NAYN ah-TIL-kuh-kee.

21. That's dangerous.

22. That's not allowed.

21. Yikh ah-deh-geh-GNAH nohw.

22. Yikh kil-KIL nohw.

10. Important Words and Phrases

1. Yes

2. No

3. Hello

4. Goodbye

5. How are you?

1. AH-oh

2. Ah-AY

3. Seh-LAHM

4. Chow

5. (B) Ehn-deh-MIN AH-lekh?
   (G) Ehn-deh-MIN AH-lesh?

6. Good

7. Bad

8. I'm sorry.

9. I don't understand.

10. I don't know.

11. Can you show me?

12. Do you understand?

6. TIH-roo

7. MEHT-foh

8. Yih-kir-TAH

9. Ahl-GEH-bah-GNIM

10. Ahl-OW-kim

11. (B) Tah-sah-yay-GNAH-lekh?
    (G) Tah-sah-yay-GNAH-lesh?

12. (B) Gehb-toh-HAHL?
    (G) Gehb-toh-SHAHL?

13. Please

14. Thank you.

15. You're welcome.

16. Excuse me.

17. My name is...

18. What is your name?

19. Here

13. (B) Eh-bah-KIKH
    (G) Eh-bah-KISH

14. Ah-meh-seh-guh-NAH-loh.

15. Mih-NIM EYE-dehl.

16. (B) Yih-KIR-tah ahr-geh-LEEGN.
    (G) Yih-KIR-tah ahr-gee-LEEGN.

17. Sih-MAY...

18. (B) SIH-mekh mahn ee-BAH-lahl?
    (G) SIH-mesh mahn ee-BAH-lahl?

19. Eh-ZEEKH

20. There

21. Where

22. Yesterday

23. Today

24. Tomorrow

25. Big

26. Small

20. Eh-ZAH

21. Yeht

22. Tih-NAHNT

23. ZAH-ray

24. NEH-geh

25. TIH-lihk

26. TIH-nish

11. People

1. We are a family.

2. This is our grandma.

3. This is our grandpa.   .

4. This is our aunt.

5. This is our uncle.

6. Friend

7. Teacher

1. Ee-GNAH beh-teh-SEHB negn.

2. Ah-yah-tah-CHIN naht.

3. Ah-yah-tah-CHIN nohw.

4. Ah-kih-stah-CHIN nech.

5. Ah-goh-tah-CHIN nohw.

6. Gwah-DAY-gnah

7. Ah-steh-mah-REE

12. Places

1. Room

2. School

3. House

4. Church

5. Park

6. Store

1. Kih-FEHL

2. Tih-MIRT bayt

3. Bayt

4. BAY-teh kris-tih-AHN

5. Mehz-NAH-gnah BOH-tah

6. Sook

7. This is your room.

8. This is your school.

9. This is our house.

10. This is our church.

11. This is the park.

12. This is the store.

7. (B) Yikh kih-FLIH nohw.
   (G) Yikh kih-FLISH nohw.

8. (B) Yikh yahn-TEH tih-MIRT bayt nohw.
   (G) Yikh yahn-CHEE tih-MIRT bayt nohw.

9. Yikh bay-tah-CHIN nohw.

10. Yikh Yeh-GNAH BAY-teh
    kris-tih-AHN nohw.

11. Yikh mehz-NAH-gnah boh-TAH nohw.

12. Yikh sook nohw.

13. We're going to your room.

14. We're going to your school.

15. We're going to our house.

16. We're going to our church.

13. (B) Wuh-DAH ahn-TEH kih-FEHL
      ee-yeh-HEH-din nohw.
    (G) Wuh-DAH ahn-CHEE kih-FEHL
      ee-yeh-HEH-din nohw.

14. (B) Wuh-DAH ahn-TEH tih-MIRT bayt
      ee-yeh-HEH-din nohw.
    (G) Wuh-DAH ahn-chee tih-MIRT bayt
      ee-yeh-HEH-din nohw.

15. Wuh-DAH bayt ee-yeh-HEH-din nohw.

16. Wuh-DAH BAY-teh kris-tih-AHN
    ee-yeh-HEH-din nohw.

17. We're going to the park.

18. We're going to the store.

17. Wuh-DAH mehz-NAH-gnah boh-TAH
    ee-yeh-HEH-din nohw.

18. Wuh-DAH sook ee-yeh-HEH-din nohw.

13. Animals

1. This is our.....

2. Dog

3. Cat

4. Fish

5. Bird

6. He won't hurt you.

1. Yikh Yeh-GNAH...nohw.
(insert type of animal before nohw.)

2. WIH-shah

3. DIH-met

4. AH-sah

5. Wuhf

6. (B) Eye-goh-dah-HIM.
   (G) Eye-goh-dah-SHIM.

7. She won't hurt you.

8. Please be gentle.

9. His name is...

10. Her name is...

7. (B) Aht-goh-dah-HIM.
   (G) Aht-goh-dah-SHIM.

8. (B) Eh-bah-KIKH kehs behl.
   (G) Eh-vah-KISH kehs bay.

9. Seh-MOO...nohw.
(insert name before nohw.)

10. Seh-MWAH...nohw.
(insert name before nohw.)

14. Clothes

1. Please put on your clothes.

2. Let me put on your clothes.

3. Pajamas

4. Shoes

5. Socks

1. (B) Eh-bah-KIKH lib-sih-HEN lih-behs.
   (G) Eh-bah-KISH lib-sheh-SHEN
       leh-beh-SHEE.

2. (B) Lah-lib-SIKH.
   (G) Lah-lib-SISH.

3. Yeh-MAH-tah libs

4. CHAH-mah

5. Kahls

6. Underwear (girls and boys)

7. Pants

8. Shirt

9. Dress

10. Jacket or coat

6. Wuhst libs

7. SOO-ree

8. SHEH-meez

9. KUH-mees

10. Koht

15. Feelings

1. Are you sad?

2. It's OK to cry.

3. Are you afraid?

4. Are you worried?

5. Are you angry?

1. (B) Ah-ZAHNK?
   (G) Ah-ZENSH?

2. Mahl-KEHS yah-LEH nohw.

3. (B) Fah-RAKH?
   (G) Fah-RAHSH?

4. (B) Teh-CHEH-nehk?
   (G) Teh-CHEH-neksh?

5. (B) Teh-NAH-dedk?
   (G) Teh-NAH-dedsh?

6. Are you happy?

7. Are you excited?

6. (B) Dehs bih-LOH-hahl?
   (G) Dehs bih-LOH-shahl?

7. (B) Dehs beh-LOH-hahl?
   (G) Dehs beh-LOH-shahl?

16. Numbers

1. One

2. Two

3. Three

4. Four

5. Five

6. Six

7. Seven

1. Ahnd

2. Hoo-LEHT

3. Sohst

4. Ah-RAHT

5. Ah-MIST

6. Sih-DIST

7. Sah-BAHT

8. Eight

9. Nine

10. Ten

11. How many?
(This can also mean: How much?)

8. Sih-MINT

9. Zeh-TEGN

10. Ah-SUHR

11. SIN-tih-nohw?

17. Colors

1. What is your favorite color?

2. Red

3. Blue

4. Green

5. Yellow

1. (B) Yeh-tee-GNOW-ehn KHAH-lehm
      nohw yah-MIT-weh-doh?
   (G) Yeh-tee-gnow-ehn KHAH-lehm
      nohw yah-MIT-wehd-jew?

2. Kye

3. Seh-mah-YAH-wee

4. Ah-rehn-GWAH-day

5. Buh-TCHAH

6. Black

7. White

8. Brown

9. Pink

10. Orange

11. Purple

6. Tih-KOHR

7. Nehch

8. BOO-nah EYE-neht

9. Rohs

10. Bir-TOO-can

11. Hahm-ROW-ee

Simple Language for Adoptive Families donates a portion of proceeds from books and CDs to improve the lives of children who wait for homes and families.

Book and CD sets are also available in Haitian Creole, Mandarin Chinese, Russian, and Spanish.

www.adoptlanguage.com